Prostitute To Pastor

ISBN: 978-0-692-99979-0

BoltonRoadPublishing@gmail.com

VI

CONTACTS:

Amy Miranda Ministries—PO Box 1442, Lodi CA 95241

Bolton Road Publishing
P.O. Box 556
Pollack Pines, CA 95726

Prostitute To Pastor

A Woman's Journey from the Spotlight to God's Light

Rev. Amy Miranda
& Darby Lee Patterson

And let the one who hears say, "Come." And let the one who is thirsty come; let the one who desires take the water of life without price.—*Revelation 22:17*

God doesn't want something from us, He simply wants us.—*C.S. Lewis*

Everyone whom the Father gives me will come to me, and the one who comes to me I will never send away.—*John 6:37*

Come now, and let us reason together, saith the Lord: though your sins be as scarlet, they shall be as white as snow; though they be red like crimson, they shall be as wool.
Isaiah 1:18

To my husband David. This book does not exist without you. Your encouragement and support to share "God's story" has allowed me to walk in freedom. I know this is part of the dream you have for us and I can't wait to see what God has around the corner.

I love you.

Acknowledgments

It's with deep gratitude that I acknowledge the following people for helping to make this book a reality: My family who always loved me, cheered me on and welcomed me home no matter where I'd been or what I'd done; Katrina and Gabriel Miranda, my precious children, for supporting and encouraging me through many years and adventures; the Miranda Family, who accepted me as a sister and loved me as one as well; Melody Phillips, my closest friend, cheerleader, supporter and the photographer for the cover of this book. I can never repay what you've done for me.

Thanks also to Anna Garza, my traveling companion through many seasons who spoke vision into my life and encouraged this book; Jana Flaig-Brummett, professional speaker and Christian humorist who has been an invaluable part of this process; to Kelly Duncan, Cheryl McEachron, and Sue Patterson, the greatest spiritual influences in my life. I am also grateful to Pastor Mark Guerrero and his wife, Gloria, who encouraged me to pursue my licensing credentials and mentored David and me in 'Ministry 101.' My Century Church family that helped shape and mold me, allowed me to use my gifts freely and loved me unconditionally. I hope I make you proud.

I also extend a thank you to Lawrence S. Daniel who believed in the value of my story, and to my co-author Darby Patterson who caught the vision and helped put it on paper. Thank you for making this journey amazing.

Foreword

It is my extreme privilege to have a small part in this project. As you read this story you will discover the power of redemption, restoration and healing. Amy's story is one of honesty, transparency and inspiration. As she details the events and choices that took her from one dark corner to another, you will discover the fulfillment of a dream that sin was not able to short circuit.

From the insecurity of a childhood that many will be able to identify with, to insurmountable odds and challenges as an adult, she brings hope and inspiration to those who may feel hopeless. This is not a comfortable story to absorb, it is filled with sadness and suffering, but the overwhelming truth of the second chance brings life and light where darkness and depravity had once ruled.

This book, like Amy's ministry will be a voice for those who have no voice or who's voice has been silenced. This work will inspire and encourage a world in need of the power of forgiveness, restoration and healing.
Amy was told when she was a child, "women don't become preachers" but God had other plans!

Pastor Mark Guerrero
Century Assemblies Church

Into the Spotlight

Ever since I was a very little girl I wanted to be a dancer. A beautiful, graceful dancer whose nimble feet glided across the floor as if floating on a cloud, freed from gravity.

My Grammy, a petite woman with short, salt and pepper hair who allowed me to do most anything I pleased, was my audience of one for performances in her living room. She'd drop a seventy-eight LP on the record player and the honey-gold voice of Tom Jones would fill the room. I'd go to the white curtains that hung over three tall windows and pull the sheers around my nine-year-old body to make a flowing gown, and dance to the music. Across the room sat an old console television and in its blank screen I saw my reflection.

A dancer. Not an awkward little girl who was always tripping on things, bumping into things. A klutz who wore thick glasses. An unremarkable, plain girl. But with the music and Tom Jones' voice, I saw a pretty and graceful girl in the TV screen. I imagined bright stage lights, an audience and the applause. Grammy understood; she was my biggest fan.

So many years later and miles away I found myself there. Under hot klieg lights, on a stage. Dancing. The soft, translucent curtains had been replaced by a revealing midnight-blue dress that could be whipped off with the flick of my wrist. My dance routine was no longer extemporaneous; it was carefully planned so that I could make the most of seductive moves that let me peel away strategic elements of my costume until I stood entirely naked in a body that had once danced in complete innocence. The audience wasn't the sweet and loving face of my Grammy, but clusters of wide-eyed men cupping their drinks and lusting for more from me and, eventually, getting it. I became a high-end escort, call-girl, stripper, and prostitute whose days and nights were fueled by drugs and alcohol.

As foreign and extreme as this experience may seem, it was far from the depths of my behavior throughout too many years of my life. Years in which a good little girl, known for her ability to excel in school and family life, left a straight and narrow highway to wander the backroads and alleys of sex, drugs and heabanging rock and roll.

This is my story. A saga that may be uncomfortable for

some people to read – though it is no longer painful for me to tell. If you will walk with me through the dark byways that paved the path to my life today as a licensed pastor, family woman and passionate promoter of change and hope, I believe you'll be inspired.

Childhood in a Bubble

Until the age of nine I was an only child living in Lawrenceburg, Indiana, with my mother – a spirited, interesting and impulsive woman. I never knew who my biological father was and I don't recalling caring. For me our relationship was entirely normal, even though there was no father in my life and my mom suffered periods of deep sadness from illness I did not understand. I was always able to focus on the positives of a life that I now know was very sheltered.

My mother would often be the source of endless excitement, planning fun activities and surprises that were out of the ordinary. I remember the night she woke me up and suggested that it would be great fun to go climb a bridge. I quickly changed out of my PJ's and we drove to the gully under the bridge that looked to me, as a child, to be as tall as a sky scraper. We climbed the scaffolding from the very bottom to the deserted street above in the moonlight. I also recall the birthday that was supposed to be snowed out by a severe and imminent storm. My mom drove to every little girl's house in her white Mustang and personally chauffeured them to our mobile home. She protected me as much as she could so that I would not be disappointed.

I made lemonade stands, built forts in the snow, went trick or treating in August and filled bags with apples instead of candy.

My memories of childhood are decorated with fun, uncommon activities designed to shelter me from the periods when home life demanded that I play the role of an adult. I remember spontaneous acts of love vividly, while the darker times seem more distant, almost as if I had only dreamed them.

There were repeated episodes in my childhood with Mom that called upon me to provide for her. She would have days of silence and withdrawal, slipping off to her room alone or burying her face in the pillows of the couch in our living room. When Mom was gone to these lonely places I'd try to make things better for her. I'd clean the kitchen, rearrange the silverware in the drawers, organize things in our house so that, when the fun-mom reappeared (as she always did), things would be just right.

There were many ups and downs in our life back then. I loved the high times and chose to focus on those. Indeed, I had a lot of help in the campaign to keep little Amy's life pleasant and protected. The adventures we had when my mom was well were intended to build a bubble around my young life and control, to the extent that my mom was able to, the happiness factor of childhood. The marvelous company of my Grammy only reinforced that I was protected and, within that prism of distorted reality, created a safe zone for me to be me. Anything I did or wanted to pretend to be, was quite fine with my Grammy – pretending to be a beauty contestant in a pageant that I would act out, or a Geisha girl with my face painted white with cold cream and wearing Grammy's scarf, or a prima ballerina in the Bolshoi Ballet. She encouraged me to play roles and let my imagination fly.

She also saw how much I loved music. How easy it was for me to get lost in its magic and leave parts of my reality behind. When I brought home a notice about my elementary school inviting students to choose their band instruments, she stopped washing dishes, wiped her soapy hands on her purple Mumu and unearthed an old trumpet she had stored in a closet. I quickly took to the instrument. When I was in middle school taking lessons and playing in the band, Grammy sat outside in her car and did crossword puzzles, patiently waiting for me. I built a group of friends within the band and we traveled by bus throughout the region to music festivals at other schools. I won many competitions. Medals and awards were tangible proof of my love for music. In my senior year, I was given the honor of being the Drum Majorette. I loved it all – the attention, the accolades and being completely surrounded by the bold music of my high school band.

I remember that my Uncle Bill came to visit us for my graduation. He'd been a professional trumpeter but had not played in many years. He made a very special memory for me when he sat down on our back-porch steps and played his trumpet with me. When I graduated, I was awarded a partial college scholarship based on my musical abilities. My plan was to attend Ball State University in Indiana and become a music teacher.

My mother's younger sister, Cindy, also protected me with weekends at her home in Cincinnati. We gobbled down popcorn while watching The Donny and Marie Osmond show on television and, knowing my love of performing, bought me a Donny and Marie microphone so that I could sing along with the radio. She sat still and let me style her hair as we watched The Carol Burnett Show. We played trumpet together, went ice skating and toured the big city together.

All this happened as an antidote, a bubble of beauty, designed to lighten the load of my mother's mood swings and my obsessive desire to make things right by organizing, cleaning, and taking on responsibility that I didn't know was unusual for a child my age. I realize now that Grammy and Aunt Cindy were protecting me. Allowing me to escape into whatever musical story I chose to make up. To imprint my childhood with happy memories. And, it worked.

I learned to jump into activities that let me pretend to be someone else. When we played 'house,' I ran the house; when my dolls were ill or hurt, I went to extremes to make them well with homemade plaster casts for broken bones and an IV drip fashioned from a personal hygiene bag.

Whatever childhood fantasy I acted out – I was in charge.

I had a special childhood friend named Erik who was on the receiving end of my bossy-pants approach. He'd come over just wanting to ride bikes, but I'd turn our play into a family tableau. I made a pretend school on my porch, complete with little desks, teaching materials and dolls. His back porch I'd make our boat. I took charge of our little drama and when I was satisfied I'd say, "Okay, now your job is to ride your bike!" Eric was a lot like me in other ways – the child of a teenage mother who never knew his biological father and lived in his grandmother's house.

Where else would a young girl, growing out of playing house as her ultimate fantasy, go but to a bigger stage! Not surprisingly, I gravitated toward high school theatre. As a thespian, I got to 'pretend' and get applause. Yet behind my drive to become someone else, there was a lonely child who yearned for something she didn't have.

When Mom announced that we'd soon be moving to a new house, I adapted and managed like a child twice my age. After all, I had a lot of practice since we moved four times by the time I was eight years old. The only thing missing in my perfectly constructed life was a dad I hadn't even known I missed.

It was a broken telephone in 1978 that granted my wish. The phone company dispatched a repairman who knocked on the door of our trailer and stole my mom's breath away. Steve was a handsome man with flaxen blond hair and bright blue eyes. He had a gentle manner about him and laughed easily. After he'd fixed the phone and left, Mom plotted with me to get him back. Since he responded to broken phones, we broke ours again and, this time, when he showed up to do the repair, she invited him to dinner. Mom and Steve dated and soon became a couple. I adored him and he treated me like a princess.

One day Steve came to me with a very serious expression on his face. He had one hand in his jacket pocket and reached out his other for mine. Then he pulled a delicate Silver Sweetheart Ring, set with a tiny diamond, from his pocket. He presented it to me and asked if it would be alright with me if he asked my mom to marry him. For me, it was a dream come true, a sign that in life, there was a perfect moment. Soon after their wedding, Steve filed papers and officially adopted me. I finally had a daddy.

My life did change in important ways. Soon, I had a little brother and then a sister. I was also introduced to a new religious home. Steve followed his heart and became a lay minister. He was so deeply committed to his Christian calling that he started a small church, not far from our home. The services at the Lighthouse Tabernacle were nothing like the subdued Sundays at the Catholic church I'd attended with my mom. They were impassioned, and encouraged participation of the congregation in the music and the praise. I developed a role for myself by learning to play three chords on the piano and rapping out a good rhythm on the tambourine so people could lift their voices in song and move to the music.

My mother, brother and sister sat dutifully in the front row.

It was especially exciting when guest preachers and musicians came to our Pentecostal church. They all fueled my attraction to both the church and the stage. Sometimes my dad would invite other preachers to our home for a meal. The kids were usually sent outdoors to play, but I wanted a place at the table. I wanted to hear the words, soak in the wisdom. Family evenings and weekends were spent immersed in Bible study and worship. And, with a minister for a dad, religion was our daily bread.

> They fueled my attraction to the church and to the stage.

I began to dream about my own place in this new and expressive form of Christian worship. In the back of my mind I was constructing a future, one that I shared with my dad when we were on one of our frequent fishing trips to the levy on the Ohio River. I was ten years old and already planning a life very different than the one I had. I told him I wanted to be a preacher and had seen myself in repeated dreams wearing a pure white suit, standing behind a pulpit in a huge stadium and preaching to a captivated crowd. I was bathed in the golden glow of stage lights and the power of music. It was my future. My dad's response was simple. "Women aren't preachers," he said. This dream of becoming someone, somewhere else, was not my first and certainly not my last.

Throughout those years I continued to provide the kind

of family care that was needed when my mom fell into depression. But now I had a bigger mission. It was up to me to protect my little brother and sister (both much younger than me) from those dark episodes. I made everything right. I kept the house orderly and clean. I put on a happy face for my vulnerable siblings and pretended everything was as it should be. Our life was good. We had great fun together. And our Mom was still uniquely wonderful and loving once the veil of melancholy lifted.

Surely this picture of my childhood doesn't account for the path I chose to walk once I turned eighteen. I had a mom and dad, siblings, friends and many cherished memories of childhood. In school I was very well liked because I could easily adapt to people's expectations. I was certainly the very picture of a good girl, a child who could shoulder responsibility and take care of business. In retrospect, I think it was my heightened sense of responsibility that contributed to my need to escape – in my imagination and in my vision for the future. There is no one to blame. My parents did their very best with circumstances that were beyond their control. And I responded by running away to an experience almost diametrically opposed to my upbringing.

A Woman on the Move

The yearning for freedom, the need to live in a world of my own making, blossomed after my high school graduation. It started in innocent ways when I was a senior in high school. I attended parties with friends, not drinking, but carefully watching and absorbing the vibe of independence in darkened rooms where forbidden things might happen. But soon, observation led to participation and I loved the way alcohol made me feel.

By then, we'd moved eight times and 'moving' was in my blood. It seemed like a solution to problems. At eighteen, I was yearning to break free and entirely unaware of what I was running from. I just needed to move. I think my mother understood because that year she let me move to Denver, Colorado, to live with Aunt Cindy and her husband.

The accepted plan was for me to live in Colorado for a year to make residency, get a job and attend college there, but my motivation was to have the freedom to party. My aunt and uncle were happy to host good Amy. Once again, I found that I was the center of someone's world, the star of my own show, inside my beautiful bubble.

My reputation for being a very good girl provided cover for me as I sought out adventure, independence. I found it in the person of a married man who was a coworker at the phone company where I'd found a part time job. He was suave and sophisticated, tall with black, wavy hair and a neat mustache. His dark, Hispanic complexion framed bright white teeth and deep penetrating brown eyes. He wore tasteful gold jewelry. He was also forty years old and married. I was so trusted by my aunt and uncle that they never suspected the nature of my relationship with the man who often dropped me off at their home. But good Amy harbored a secret, unknown even to herself, and her life was about to take a radical turn down a rocky road.

Not only did my 'lover' provide graduate level sex education for a girl who'd just turned eighteen, he was also my guide to the cocaine kingdom. Through it all, he flattered me and made me forget that I was a scrawny, gangly girl from Indiana. I felt like I was under a spotlight, a shining little, dancing star. In exchange, I gave him my innocence which he accepted like a lascivious glutton.

Somewhere in my young, confused mind, I knew this affair was destined to end badly and I fled Colorado within the year. Mom and dad had moved to Florida. Unlike Lawrenceburg, Indiana, population about five thousand, Florida sounded big, metropolitan, sophisticated. A 'State' of possibilities. I knew from experience that moving could solve problems. So, I admitted to my parents that I'd been involved with drugs and was still accepted back into their fold. Of course, out of their sight I continued to party.

Almost immediately I learned that, in Florida, so long as I didn't drink, it was okay for me as a nineteen-year-old to be in bars and nightclubs. My underage stature was indicated by a special wristband that prevented me from buying drinks. But there was plenty of drinking before I went and after I left the bar. And, there were so many other things I could do in those dark bars that the absence of alcohol was unimportant! I became a chameleon and adapted to the seductive rock and roll environment. I colored my hair so that one-half was white and the other black. I wore a big metal key in my pierced ear. I entered the wet tee-shirt contests at the bar and reveled in the spotlight.

While hanging out in random apartments, my new friends did not encourage me to participate when drugs were being passed around. No, it was me being in charge of myself, who one day decided to give crank a try. Crank is a powerful stimulant that acts on the central nervous system. It's a derivative of Methamphetamine (Meth) that has lower purity and is taken as a powder. I was learning to favor drugs that brought on an immediate high, euphoria and an energy rush. Of course, the cost of this high was extreme lows during withdrawal, and a very troubled Amy in my parent's home. When I'd left for Colorado I was Amy the good girl listening to Tom Jones and Englebert Humperdink; now I was gyrating to the beat of Guns and Roses.

Naturally, this behavior overwhelmed the ability of my parents to have me living with them. I moved into a house with some girls I'd met on my nightly trips to the bar and we built a life of nonstop partying. I did know that I would need a job to survive and support my life style. Since I had no useful training or education, I reached back into my childhood and, once again, the precious time I spent with my Grammy came to my rescue. Knowing how much I loved to dance, she would put my little feet on hers and teach me ballroom dance steps in her living room. Not formal training, certainly, but enough to land me a job as a ballroom dance teacher. I soon learned the job was about far more than dancing, and it taught me skills that I was able to incorporate in other aspects of my life as I wandered far from the path of childhood. Chief among those lessons was the art of manipulation. Dance studios make money and build customer loyalty by upselling. They appeal to the vanity and ego of clients who are simply thrilled to believe they have extraordinary talent. I would gain the admiration of my dance partner and then deliver the pitch. "You know, we don't usually allow our clients to skip levels in our dance program," I'd confide. "But you I think we could advance to the Gold Level just because you've really got what it takes!" Most often it was an easy sell. What wasn't easy was doing work that required a sharp mind and an energetic body. After partying all night, I realized I wasn't up to the daily challenge of teaching and selling. I needed something mindless, not demanding, because it was more important to me to live the high life than to build a good life.

Like a bottom feeder in a fish tank, I sought out the lowliest position that I could find. A job with few expectations and requiring no skill beyond getting up and going to work every day. I got a repetitive, mindless factory job. I was very surprised to discover that my job making bed springs there was still too much for me. It was greasy, dirty and exhausting, and required physical labor that was beyond my ability to deliver. I made it through one paycheck and quit.

My inability to hang onto even a menial job because of my life style, reached some part of my consciousness. I felt as if my life was over unless I made a radical change and, for me, not much was more radical than joining the Armed

Forces. I tried to clean up my act and marched off to the nearby Air Force recruiting office. I was feeling pretty good about the testing and interviews I'd had, and we were well into the process when the recruiter said he needed to ask me some "protocol questions." Among the first question was, "Have you ever done drugs?" The good little Amy didn't lie and I said, "Yes, I have." He then asked what kind of drugs I'd done and gave him a short list – LSD, cocaine, mushrooms. He stopped me there and apologized. "Sorry, we can't accept you." I argued that I had stopped doing drugs and, maybe feeling some sympathy for me, the recruiter quietly suggested that I maybe should try the Navy, since their requirements might not be so rigid.

That rejection catapulted me back into 'the life.' I moved in with a drug dealer who had lots of other girls living in the house. I used cocaine every day, every night. Wild sex went along with it. Once, I overdosed on coke and was so buzzed that I jumped out of a moving car. At the same time, my room in the house was decorated with posters of my favorite ballet dancer, Mikhail Baryshnikov. I also had a pair of satin ballet slippers hanging on a hook near my bed. These vestiges of 'good Amy' stood in stark contrast to my lifestyle.

Those months in Florida quickly became a blur of drugs, sex and disappointment. I got involved with a guitar player who went for kinky sex, had the experience of other women being included in those cocaine-fueled escapades, contracted a venereal disease from a guy I barely knew, and was visited by my high school sweetheart who came to take me back to Indiana and have a life with him. He soon found I wasn't the same girl he'd known years ago - the good little Amy. He left after just one week.

I went to my mother, as I often did while wandering through my maze of wrong turns. I complained that even the Armed Forces wouldn't have me. Like many times before, my mom suggested that a move might turn things around. She said a friend's daughter had relocated to New York and that might be good for me as well. New York, like Frank Sinatra sang, "the top of the heap!" I did manage to land on the top of the heap, but not the one depicted in the song.

Big City, Bright Lights, Big Lies

New York was worlds away from Lawrenceburg where the good little Amy had spent her childhood. It was far more cosmopolitan than Florida and vastly bigger than Denver. I could get lost there. And I did.

I finally had my chance at being a professional dancer. Of course, it wasn't for the New York Ballet but, instead, at bachelor parties. These male bonding celebrations put me center stage and I learned to make the most of it. I wore costumes that teased the imagination; I developed my own dance routines and I learned how to really entertain. The more I did it, the easier it became. In those homes and hotel rooms I was the star attraction; popular and famous in a world of my own making. The attention made me feel attractive, even beautiful. After a childhood of being awkward and dorky-looking the response to my stripping at bachelor parties became a drug in itself. I wanted more, needed more. My old companion, cocaine, fueled all my creativity and energy, and alcohol helped me loosen up. I made extra money by favoring the groom with oral sex.

With few exceptions, I never felt in danger. I had developed a friendly relationship with a cab driver named Emery – he told me I reminded him of his own daughter, perhaps seeing behind the mask I wore when being taken to one of the bachelor engagements. He always waited in his taxi for me to finish the night's engagement. One night, when far too much alcohol was consumed, the groomsmen decided they would all have a piece of me. The drunken and determined looks on their faces left me no doubt about how far they would go. They fixed their eyes on me and moved in, grabbing and groping as I struggled to get away. Emery sensed I'd been gone too long and burst in the door to rescue me, picked me up and carried me out. Even with that experience, I continued to show up to entertain at bachelor parties - the young revelers made me feel like a shooting star.

The success I'd had in these private venues led me to seek a bigger stage. The attention I got at the bachelor parties fed me something I needed. It seemed a long way from the ugly and scrawny girl who'd had one boyfriend in eighteen years. The bachelor party boys let me feel beautiful. And when some of the guys at a bachelor party I'd done said that I must be from Canada because I was so good, they set up my expectation that Canada was an even loftier stage for my ambitions.

My next step took me down yet another rung on the ladder of self-respect, though then, I saw it as moving up. I decided to become an exotic dancer. I even sought the blessing of my mom who came to visit me in New York and went to the club where I intended to start working as a stripper. She observed that, if she were younger and had the body, it might be a great place to work. She further suggested I take on the stage name of Sydney. Soon after, Sydney was stripping in night clubs, going home with the clients, staying true to her/my cocaine habit and sending money home to help out my family. With a new name, I could further divorce myself from what good Amy was becoming.

Once the excitement and allure of taking my clothes off in front of an audience was no longer enough, I upped the stakes so that I could earn more money and, at the same time, advance what I considered my career. My rationale was simple: I was already having plenty of sex with various men and I might as well get paid for it. I became an escort. Not just a call girl, but a high-end escort with a group of men known as 'clientele'.

Entry into the industry was not difficult. But I soon learned that it was far more than getting a date with someone, having sex and collecting money. I worked for a Madam, a woman who had once been an escort herself and possessed an uncanny business sense. I was put into a training program which included spending time servicing three of her oldest clients. These elder men, one by one, judged my performance and offered practical advice on how to stay safe, collect money and guard the 'integrity' of the business. Once Madam was satisfied, I started getting calls for my services. I kept her attention and, soon, I was being selected for the high-end encounters. That meant beautiful hotels and clients who were wealthy, famous athletes and high-profile people.

That meant beautiful hotels and clients who were wealthy, famous athletes. and high-profile people.

The stature of these johns did not mean they were any less twisted or bizarre in their sexual appetites than the entry level 'dates.' One man asked me to come to the back door of his home where he'd leave a note for me describing the scene he would like to play out with me that day. Each encounter was a bit different, but all had one thing in common; I was to play the part of his daughter. His daughter as a grade school girl. His daughter in high school and in various childhood environments. He wanted me to call him "Daddy."

Another john wanted me to lay on a blanket on the floor while he touched me with his feet. Yet another took the kinky requests to an extreme level. Let me only report that it took place in his bathroom and, when I felt unable to comply with his wishes, had to call Madam. Not even the cocaine and alcohol that coursed through my body were enough. She stayed on the phone and talked me through the encounter.

Why did I wander to such dark places where moral boundaries faded like the edges of an airbrushed tattoo? Where almost nothing was taboo? I told myself this: I was Sydney. I'd left Amy back in Lawrenceburg. Sydney accepted the world she was in and she would make the absolute best of it. Sydney was admired and desired. As proof, I was worth $500 an hour as an escort. I dressed like a fashion queen and strode into the lobbies of New York's finest hotels with my head held high and leather briefcase in my hand. No paperwork cluttered that briefcase however. It was neatly organized with the tools of my trade – a credit card machine, lingerie, oils and condoms.

Throughout the months I spent in New York I learned to personally disconnect from the johns I serviced while, at the same time, making them feel like the sole objects of my affection. One married john was so connected that he acquired an apartment for me in Buffalo. He took me on trips and sailing on his luxurious cabin cruiser on the river. I was living the life of a trophy wife without the wedding ring. But that wasn't enough for Sydney. A friend of his also expressed interest in me and thus began a short period in which I had my own small stable of tricks, allowing me to skip paying the Madam's commission.

My married john took his own life by jumping off a building. He'd discovered he had HIV. For months I lived with the fear he's passed it on to me although that serious concern did not alter my lifestyle.

Living in New York provided the opportunity to travel, on occasion, to Canada and I had acquired a Canadian passport. My fascination with this north-of-the-border sanctuary started with the comment at that bachelor party and justified my desire to move again.

The Canada Connection

I auditioned at a night club in Niagara Falls, Canada, and won my place in their lineup of dancers, known to the outside world as strippers. I loved the fact that I'd had to audition to perform on their huge stage. I felt like I'd "made it." I was a genuine show girl. I'd made that happen. It was not given to me or created for me.

We were paid regular wages and danced for tips. There was a hierarchy to this off-beat industry and all the features of a legitimate business. There were bosses, money managers, a supply chain, security and talent management – all dedicated to making money from women like me taking their clothes off.

The stage was T-shaped and where we'd do our solo dance in rotation. At the foot of the stage were half-booths that offered some privacy. If a guy liked your dance on stage he'd request a personal dance. There was also a back room that provided even more privacy, for a price. Lots of special requests meant a dancer was very good and I, of course, wanted to be in that elite club. I worked very hard on my dance routines. I learned how to coordinate my stripping moves and dance steps. I used props to make the performance more interesting. In the minutes that I commanded the stage and all eyes were on me, I felt like a professional. Like I had some value and worth.

I was also part of an underground and informal sorority of sisters. We shared tricks of the trade, like what to do when your period came – answer, use a tampon with the string cut off. This tip led to my most embarrassing moment when I discovered I'd forgotten to trim the string and had danced my routine with it dangling between my legs. From the other girls, I learned how to do gimmicks for our clients like pealing back a matchstick till it's flat, licking it so that it sticks on the nipples, lighting it and singing Happy Birthday. Dancers also shared the excitement of a visit from the traveling salesmen that specialized in the tools of our trade. His trunk held pasties, feather boas, wigs and high heeled shoes. We ate chicken fingers and French fries together and changed each other's piercings. When we sat alone at the bar we spoke about family life and talked about God. Some of the strippers were college girls trying to get by, and out of the game. Others were lifers, though the professional life was bound to be short. We lived in a small world of our own making. There was no judgment, only a sense of belonging – something I needed.

In Canada, it was a mix of regular Joes and wealthy men, some well-known. There were professional athletes, sharply dressed businessmen and more than a few politicians. Unlike the U.S., Canada allows strippers to be completely naked and security guys hung out on the edges, watching for signs of trouble. The most frequent behavior that got customers booted out was masturbating while we gyrated on the stage.

Despite my little community of 'sisters' and the status of the venue, I became restless and decided to move on. My destination was St. Catharines, north of Niagara and one of Ontario's largest cities. As a performance venue, I saw it as a kind of downgrade. The stage was much smaller than the one in Niagara, it was darker and lacked the pizzazz. On the other hand, it had a homey feel and a fifty-year-old Greek owner named Stavros with the qualities of a favorite uncle.

But it was another employee who drew my closest attention. Dino was the dee-jay who provided the music for the dancers and filled my heart with yearning. Dino was a storyteller. A man who could smoothly spin a yarn and take you where he wanted you to go. Dino made me laugh. Years before he'd been hit by a bocci ball and had broken out a front tooth. He'd take out the replacement tooth and beam a smile at the girls, looking like a happy jack-o-lantern. He spoke fluent French, English and (being part of a big family with roots in Naples) Italian. Dino played the music that was expected in a strip joint, but in private his favorite recording artist was John Lennon. He was a man with so much personality that his short stature and less than matinee-idol looks were inconsequential. Of course, there was another side to Dino. A rough side, a little threatening tone, but I fell for him completely.

> Six months later I found out that I was pregnant.

I found that I no longer needed my daily cocaine, though I continued to drink. Cocaine had been my source of courage and energy. With Dino in my life, I discovered I had a well of courage of my own. We went out for great French meals together; he took me to meet his pure Italian family.

Six months later, I found out that I was pregnant. Dino did not welcome the news and advised an abortion. He felt (rightly so) that a strip bar would be no place to raise a child. Right then, some whisper from good Amy reached my soul and I made a decision. Since I knew Dino's anger and it frightened me, I told him I needed the comfort of my mom to help me through a procedure. I had already decided my baby would be born and I bought a round trip Amtrak, knowing I wouldn't be using the return portion. Rightly or not, I feared his retribution even though I would be in Florida 1,000 miles away.

My second try at life in Florida was unsuccessful. My mother had divorced Steve after eleven years of marriage. He'd been unfaithful and neither one could move past it. Mom had remarried and, in my mind, had made a terrible choice. Once again, my Grammy, who had moved out to California, rescued me. She learned about my dilemma and bought me a one-way ticket to her door. I wish I could say that marked the end of my career as an exotic dancer, but I took one last job at a strip club in Florida before my pregnancy showed. I wanted to earn enough money so that my little brother could enjoy a really nice birthday. The next day I boarded the plane to California, grateful for the rescue. And deeply uncertain about my future.

Journey into the Light

I moved to Lodi, California, in 1990 and decided to turn my life around. The first question I'd had when I accepted Grammy's offer was, "Will I have to go to church?"

I settled in and adjusted to life with my Grammy who was at my side throughout my pregnancy – attending Lamaze classes and taking me to the hospital when the baby girl decided to be born. When it came time for the delivery, I wouldn't let Grammy talk to me or help me through the exercises we'd learned in the classes. I just wanted her presence. I wanted to stare at her and simply have her be there for me. Katrina was born beautiful and perfect at seven pounds, six ounces. From that moment on, I knew where the focus of my life would be.

With Grammy's emotional support, I was living off welfare and attending school to become a dental assistant. At the same time, Grammy would hold events for her church groups at her home, and I took notice. I believed that church was no place for a woman as 'broken' as myself, but there was a chance for Katrina, in her innocence, to be part of something that would help guide and inform her life. So, when she was six months old, I started to attend Century Church in Lodi, for my daughter since I was, I thought, beyond redemption.

The world that I'd been lost in for more than five years was one in which there can be no hopes or dreams. I was in another bubble and, unlike the one I'd grown up in, it was not safe or beautiful. I knew that I would die young and alone either from alcohol, an accident or by someone's hand. I did not want my daughter exposed to Sydney's world.

Century Church had a lovely choir and, as always, music called to me. I asked the choral director if I could join the music ministry even though I no longer considered myself the Christian I once was. I knew that, despite my own doubts about religion, I could, as I always had, blend in. The director's wife took me under her wing and helped me to integrate my own lost voice into the choir of praise. That Wednesday, I attended my first rehearsal with the group and felt good about my return to music, though guarded around other members who never needed to know the path that brought me into their fold. This was no place, I knew, for the darkness of my past to be revealed. That next Sunday, I learned just how wrong I was.

I cannot recall the exact message that the pastor delivered on the day of my turning point and, perhaps, I was not meant to hang onto his powerful words. Something in that thirty-minute sermon reached deep inside me, beyond words or rational thought and touched my sleeping spirit. I felt a combination of panic and bliss, as if broken pieces of my soul were falling back into place and there was hope of being made whole.

In his message, I heard a truth that had been lost to me – The Easter Story was my story, everyone's story. Jesus died, not just for the powerful and wealthy, but for the broken. For people like me. He rose from his darkest days and hours to be embraced by God's love and light. That same light could fall on a person like me.

I felt the burden of my past lift like a cloud. I knew in that moment that I didn't have to "fix my life," but only surrender to the new path being laid out before me. I rose from my seat and answered the Altar Call. I fell to my knees and sobbed, letting the tears wash away my guilt and shame. I prayed to God, "I have made a mess of my life and I don't know what you will do with me, but I put myself in your hands." Like unformed pieces of clay waiting for the hands of a master sculptor, I trusted God to make something beautiful of broken Amy. I knew I was about to begin the most beautiful journey ever, and I'd just taken the first step.

The choir became a spiritual home, not only for the music that never failed to move me, but also for the friends I made there – people walking beside me, imperfect like me and seeking to live in God's light. One of the women suggested there was a man she'd like me to meet, a man named David. My response was that I needed a man like I needed a hole in my head! David had already done his homework on me, coming to church to spot me in choir – the one with the spiked short hair, and, though he favored long hair, figured that detail was not a deal breaker.

> His name was written on my heart. David.

I met him at Red Robin in Stockton with three other couples. We got along just fine and I felt a gentle spark of interest in this man. Later, we went to the home of one couple to play board games. David and I were paired on the same team when we both reached for a game piece at the same time, his hand brushed mine. I felt it immediately, a sense of completion. His name was written on my heart. I went home and told Grammy I'd just met the man I was going to marry.

David was older than me at thirty-six to my twenty-three. I discovered later that he was concerned about this age gap. That is, until I told him a bit about my past as a stripper. He accepted my confession with grace, saying that my having lived such a life meant I'd sowed all my wild oats. As for me, I knew I'd found a responsible, mature man unlike any I'd ever known. We fell in love.

David treated me like the Amy I deeply wanted to be. He let me feel that I didn't have to "settle" anymore as our affection for each other grew. I believe the real awakening to the fact that I'd finally stepped on a righteous path came with a phone call I received from Dino while I was on a date with David. Not knowing that I wasn't alone and vulnerable, Dino became very angry and shouted threats at me on that call. Instead of cowering as I'd done so many times in the past, I told him loud and clear to never, ever call me again. I had with me at that moment, a man of conscious who walked in God's light and I intended to be by his side. I had awaked to my new life. Sydney was silenced and gone forever.

It was about three months later, at a celebration after the Christmas production at the church, that I learned the true depth of our relationship. The choir director was at the mic and had asked people to share their stories. David stood and went to the microphone. He looked over the crowd and then at me. "Amy Lewis," he said, "will you marry me?" He pulled a ring from his pocket and I sobbed, "yes."

I later learned that one of David's initial hesitations

about meeting me had been his intent to not marry someone who already had a child. Then, he heard a sermon at a church in Sacramento in which the speaker had talked about accepting someone else's child as one's own. "What if Joseph had said that about Mary?" he'd asked, and David changed his mind. David had then agreed to meet me and, after our marriage in 1992, Katrina became 'our' daughter.

From Shadows to Light

Having David accept me and my past – at least the part I'd told him about - became a keystone for each new day. With his constant affirmation of my flawed self, and the new clarity I felt in my relationship with God, I knew my life was forever changed. But at the same time, something was holding me back from walking the Christian path with full confidence. Of course, I knew what it was. I'd told David only a partial truth about my past, the part that didn't seem quite so awful. The part about my exotic dancing. The rest I'd boxed up and stored in the dark corners of my mind. For five years I lived with this secret, so happy with my marriage and church life that I just didn't want to risk bursting my pretty new bubble. When a memory from that hidden place awakened and teased at my mind I pushed it back into the shadows and willed it to sleep. But of course, those experiences were very much alive in my memory and sought the light, time and again. It was an uncomfortable and conditional peace in which I lived.

I felt even more deceptive when our church launched rehearsals for an Easter play; a play in which I was to have the part of a prostitute. There, in front of our congregation and God, I sat and gave the character's moving and deeply felt testimony. I received the compliments afterwards with a complex of emotions. I alone knew the reason why I'd give such an authentic performance as a prostitute. And I alone knew that I could not wear that same mask into my Christian life for much longer.

Throughout those years, I kept up my momentum for change. For the first few, it wasn't so hard to not focus on myself. In 1993, our son Gabriel was born and required a lot of our attention. He has a rare genetic disorder, Chromosome 15 Prader-Willie Syndrome, that causes several growth and development delays. People with the syndrome often have an insatiable appetite, as well as possible intellectual impairment and obsessive behaviors that need ongoing management. Many do not make it through infancy and for several weeks we were not sure he'd make it home from the hospital. Naturally, David and I were overwhelmed and confused. And, even more naturally, I wondered if Gabe's condition was retribution for the kind of life I'd lived. But with David's help, I came to know that caring for Gabe, learning about the potential for his life and bringing him through his many challenges would only speak to our better angels. We would grow to be more kind and compassionate, to ourselves and to others. I called upon my childhood resilience and decided to be the very best mother possible for the blessed child we'd received.

As any parent with a special needs child knows, the day-to-day challenges are many. In the very beginning, we were unsure our baby boy would make it through the repeated testing, survive frailties that come with Prader-Willie Syndrome, and make it to his fifth birthday. In the back of our minds, of course, were many unknowns. How severely would his intellectual abilities be affected; what physical limitations would he have? Would he need braces for his legs? Would he be bullied and would he have friends?

David and I called upon our faith and belief that there would be a good outcome in Gabe's different, but valuable life. I feel that he awakened our compassion for others and taught us so many lessons that we can now share with others. He was born, as we all are, with God's purpose. Gabe is now a young man who, with medical and cognitive challenges, surpassed expectations for his own quality of life and make us far better people.

By 1996, we'd developed a rhythm in our family life and I was able to help out financially with a job as a teaching assistant at a church school. In the first week of my employment, one of the teachers left to attend to family matters and

I was asked to step in as a substitute. Teaching that first grade class was like breathing for me – so natural and affirming. I started taking classes at Cosumnes River College to learn more about early childhood education. The following school year, I returned as a teacher's aide but was quickly asked to take over the teaching post in the kindergarten class, replacing a woman who had a Master's Degree but little affinity for small children.

At the private school, it was possible for a small percentage of teachers who proved their worth, to be exempt from the credentialing requirement. Later, a beautiful door opened for me at a Christian school in Elk Grove, leading to additional teaching posts in a variety of subjects including American Sign Language – a skill acquired so that we could communicate with Gabe, who was able to hear but unable to speak until he was five years old.

I loved it all – the children and music and feeling good about my life.

I loved it all – the children and music and feeling good about my life. I stayed busy, too busy, I hoped, for the guilty memories to occupy my mind for more than a few fleeting moments. Were it not for the fact that those memories would never be truly gone because they were (and are) part of my life experience, my busyness might have worked. However, I found out just how much the truth wanted to be in the light of day when I attended a Christian women's retreat at a church in the Sierra foothills.

In the presence of so many women, all walking the same path to live in God's light, I found my courage in truth. I was inspired and challenged by the talks and activities at the conference and I was brimming with hope. I was ready for a transformation when a woman named Edie Patterson called me to her side and quietly asked me if I'd ever done any witchcraft. I could honestly answer that I'd not engaged in that particular, dark magic. She looked at me with curiosity and kindness, and said that something was holding me back. She placed her hand on my forehead and prayed.

God's touch flowed through her warm hands and into my being, through my body, into my heart and my troubled soul; past my new pretending and into the dark corners of imprisoned memories. He showered me with healing light and my fears surrendered. When she called the name "Jesus," I felt His powerful presence and fell to the floor, blessed with acceptance and God's love. I felt completely embraced, inside and out. Clean and new.

Back at home I summoned my courage and told David

the truth, all of it. I felt tempted to soften the reality by calling myself "a lady of the night," but knew that would create another veil to be lifted. I'd been a prostitute. I'd sold my innocence and my body for money and attention. I'd done most of those assignations heavily under the influence of drugs and alcohol. And, oh yes, as I'd already admitted to David, I'd been a stripper, but one who also received tips for special sexual favors. There was no way to pretty-up the bare reality of my adult life before God drew me into his family.

As an affirmation of the new path I'd chosen to walk, David responded with Christian love and charity. He expressed sympathy for the pain I'd experienced. Sorrow for the years I'd been so lost. And then, as if a page had been turned, said, "Babe, you have to share this. You have to tell other people what you've been through. Think of the people you can help!"

David went from forgiveness to salvation, from shame to hope, in one encompassing statement. I immediately heard and understood. Just moments before, my heart was heavy and weighted with secrets I'd locked in the dark. Exposed to the light, they were no longer a burden. In fact, I understood I would use my past and the story of how God had helped me turn my life around, to help others trapped by regret and shame. I would give them hope.

I started in small ways, sharing parts of my story with a small group of women from the church. Gradually, the gatherings grew more public and larger. I was invited to speak at other venues – churches, homes and gathering places. I met a woman named Jana, a friend, inspirational humorist and professional speaker, who invested her time to help me refine my message and presentations. David said he envisioned the day when we'd travel together in our bus, changing lives through God's love. Me, telling my story and bringing His message to women all over, and David, by my side and selling my book. People, places and opportunities aligned in my life and I felt ready to officially launch Amy Miranda Ministries.

People, places and opportunities aligned in my life and I felt ready to officially launch Amy Miranda Ministries.

Others who heard my message also gave me important support. In particular, Melody Phillips, my best friend and professional singer, offered her home as a venue for groups of five or six women to come and hear my testimony. Month after month the gatherings grew and when twenty-five women showed up, we knew it was time to move along to a greater public venue. When I told my story to more than five -

hundred women at a conference, God's plan for my life was clear. I had an opportunity to help countless women rise from shame and guilt, and walk in their own God-given light.

David has been beside me every step of the way, traveling with me, caring for our children, helping me to prepare for my presentations and always reminding me that I am loved – consistently and unconditionally.

A Woman's Way

As I've traveled to churches and gatherings of Christian women, I've seen miracles happen. I've been present when women burdened by a secret past have opened their hearts to the light of God's love and purpose, changing the course of their lives forever. How does this happen?

As women, we are born to carry. We carry our babies in the womb, the heart and arms. We are the gatherers. We gather sustenance for our families and carry the bundles to our home and hearth. We are the bearers of nourishment. We are steady and able to bear the weight we carry in fulfilling our role as women.

But as we carry these life sustaining loads we also learn to bear things that simply weigh us down and provide no great benefit to survival or happiness. Women carry guilt, regret, resentment and shame. We share it with no one. It's stored in the dark where it grows and multiples like a mold, never being exposed to light that heals. Let me explain how I've learned to understand how this instinct prevents us from living the life God intended for us:

Jeremiah 29:11 says that God has a plan for us, given to us from the moment of birth. Because God is good, the plan offers only benefit for us. Hope, love, a future and a purpose. He knows us from the moment of conception and our growth in the womb.

His design is who we were born to be. But because we are also born with responsibility, He does not lay out our path before us, a path that may have many exits and obstacles. We might see our circumstances (our family, health, economic status) and feel a hopelessness that erodes our trust in God. Let me give you this personal example:

My childhood was protected by denial of my mother's clinical depression. I became lost in the fantasy that, through organizing, cleaning, directing and putting on a happy face, everything would be fine. My Grammy sheltered me and helped me vanish into imagined realities and 'other worlds.' There is no blame in this revelation. I know they both intended only good. But I became a chameleon – able to change into whatever Amy I needed to be to suit the circumstances.

And, I had my whole life figured out. I would be a music teacher and a part-time preacher. After all, no little girl grows up planning to be a stripper dancing to recorded music!

By the time I graduated from high school, I grew to believe that I was in charge. When life didn't unfold as I thought it should, I started to make compromises. Doubt of God's presence in my life crept into my immature mind. With alcohol, drugs and male attention, I eventually quieted God's gentle voice, almost entirely.

I believed that if I could get the trappings of a successful life, that would be enough. The clothes, fine hotels, fancy restaurants, and wealthy and flattering johns. But like buying a knock-off Coach handbag that's a shabby substitute for the quality and workmanship of the real thing, my 'chosen' life started to disintegrate – zipper broke, lining tore and leather shredded. There was nothing genuine about the life I was building and it was miles away from the road that God had laid out for me.

In Canada, when I hooked up with Dino, God gave me the chance that turned my life around. I became pregnant. And, as lost as I was, there was path I would not, could not walk. Abortion was not even a possibility. I was threatened and harassed, but took myself and the baby I was carrying to salvation.

Romans 8:28 says "All things work together for good to them that love God." And, although I had to walk many miles to accept my own awakening, I made the journey. I know that life isn't always fair and is sometimes downright hurtful. But these trials can bring us closer to God, instead of chasing us away.

As a woman, it was exceptionally hard for me to lay down the burdens I'd carried for so many years. But when I finally exposed my past to God's light, the shame and guilt lifted like a dense fog gives way to the sun.

I am not ashamed to tell people about the path I followed toward God's light. I often compare it to being weighted down with a backpack filled with rocks. Each rock is inscribed with an emotion – shame, guilt, regret, resentment, bitterness. (Please, add your own labels to your own rocks). As women, we lean forward with hunched shoulders under the weight, while the backpack protects our secrets from the rest of the world. We are so accustomed to the daily burden that we barely realize we are carrying anything at all.

At the same time, we view ourselves as broken. Once, when we were born, we were a beautiful masterpiece painted onto a fragile tile, a tile we've broken into hundreds of little pieces. We have forgotten that Romans 5:8 tells us "I loved you at your darkest," and believe that God cannot possibly accept us for who we are, where we are. However, the opposite is true, and God showed us that through the suffering and sacrifice of his own son.

God doesn't wait for us to go clean ourselves up. He loves us as we are. He waits for as long as it takes. He welcomes the authentic you. There is no need to carry the burden on your back or to feel broken.

I remember the day when I took the heavy rocks of my own shame and guilt from my back and placed them in the light. As the weight lifted from my body I was able to stand with my head up and shoulders back, arms open to embrace all that God had given me. As Jerimiah explained, God "plans to prosper you and not to harm you, plans to give you hope and a future." Yes, life is not always fair and is certainly filled with pain. But through all these trials God has endowed us with the ability to persevere, to show strength and to rely on the inherent goodness with which he blessed us at our birth. Like our individual fingerprints, that 'soul print' given to us by God, is unique. It allows each of us to err and stray, to become discouraged or doubtful, but also to draw upon that embedded strength and faith that's uniquely ours.

Let me draw, again, from my own experience to contrast

my years of walking in the shadows and my awakening to God's light. I've already told you of the years I spent taking charge of my life, the dark and dangerous paths I wandered, and the heavy weight I carried until God finally got my attention. You would think that I'd paid some dues and suffered the consequences of taking a detour from God's path for me. But life handed me (and my husband, David) another challenge. When our son was born, his survival was greatly in doubt. Should he live, the prognosis for his life was not good. In addition, there were emotional and financial challenges that could overwhelm even the most optimistic of people.

I knew and trusted that Gabe's birth and life would bring us closer to God ...

But by then, I'd opened my heart to God's love and owned his soul print for me. I knew and trusted that Gabe's birth and life would bring us closer to God in ways I could not predict. Instead of indulging in self-pity, David and I believed this special baby was part of God's plan. His plan is always good, never punishing. We forged ahead with love and faith.

What a difference God's light makes! Nurturing our son to adulthood has given me so many gifts. I shudder to think what might have happened had I not returned to church, for the sake of my daughter only, because (I believed) I was far too damaged for God to accept. But I learned that God had a purpose for me and was only waiting for me to surrender.

I accepted His invitation, and soon more opportunities appeared. I was asked to serve as vice principal at the Century Church School in Lodi, helping to revive the school's curriculum and quality. In the second year, I became acting Principal and then an Associate Pastor. In 2017, I achieved my lifetime goal and became a credentialed pastor, Reverend Amy Miranda. What an amazing, winding path from dark rooms of my past to classrooms filled with love and light, and a church that's become my spiritual home.

The life of Jesus is the story of God's intention. His Son came for the sick and the broken. He came for the life that was shattered like so many pieces of painted tile. That was me. That morning I surrendered my life to Christ, He took those broken pieces and reassembled them. He made them something beautiful and useful, like a broken vase that has been mended to once again hold blooming flowers. He gave me purpose. My husband, my son, my daughter and my story to tell so that others might also step into the light of God's love.

Lost and Found

There is no smooth and straight highway that takes our lives from the start of our journey to its end. Along the way we encounter many exits and detours. Some we choose to explore and others we pass by. The exit I chose as an 18-year-old led me into a labyrinth of risk and danger, disguised as excitement and escape. I wandered through those dark corridors and became hopelessly lost. I could see no light in the distance to guide me. I followed the voices in my mind that told me lies about who I was and what I wanted to be.

'Finally, you're a professional dancer!'

'I'm in the spotlight and all those men admire me!'

'I'm having plenty of sex and now I get paid for it.'

'Cocaine and alcohol make me better at everything.'

'I'm in charge of my own life!'

Thankfully, God sent me a gift that let me turn a corner and escape from the dark labyrinth I'd been wandering: the life of my unborn child. Suddenly, there was a place I could not, would not go, despite threats and promises from the baby's reluctant father. I saw a beacon of light in the distance and took my first steps back onto the path God intended me to walk.

With the support of my church and my husband, I became aware of what had happened to me. So profound and important was this realization and acceptance of the truth, God's truth, that I knew I had to share it with others because, though my experience with drugs and sex and immorality seems extreme, it is certainly not unique.

This is how I now understand what can happen to us. We were born perfect. Not perfect in the eyes of others – even our parent's – but as the perfect design God made for each of us, individually. This is our authentic self.

As we move from childhood to adolescence and adulthood, we get lots of feedback from the world about who we are. It might come in the form of disapproval or abuse or neglect, or as a physical or mental challenge. We might get attention and approval from others for negative behavior. Any manner of things can happen to us that get our attention and send us messages we come to believe as truth about ourselves. Sometimes the feedback is so loud and strong we lose track of our God-given, authentic selves.

For me, I chose what I call a 'knock-off' life. I was a Gucci purse made with faux leather, a cut-glass Tiffany ring. I knew it wasn't the real thing, but I was willing to pretend. Because I was looking in all the wrong places to validate my life, I didn't realize that the Amy God made, was the genuine and valuable article! Consequently, I kept seeking out reinforcement for my inauthentic self. I went from a party dancer to a stripper, to being a prostitute. It was as if I had two wolves walking by my side – the good wolf and the bad wolf. I fed the bad wolf steak and let the other get by on scraps.

> I was a Gucci purse made with faux leather, a cut-glass Tiffany ring.

In that beautiful moment in which I accepted God's truth about my own life, I recognized both the opportunity and responsibility I'd been given. I clearly heard that there was no need to feel guilt, shame and regret. There was no benefit to waking up feeling defeated and unworthy. These thoughts draw us away from God and muffle his voice. This is not what He intends for us. This is not our authentic God -given self.

Being given these realizations created opportunity for me. I could openly accept my past without shame and share it with others who were suffering under the weight of theirs. Indeed, the more I spoke with women who had carried guilt and regret on their backs, the more convinced I was that I have a responsibility. Amy Miranda Ministries is my channel for expressing that responsibility and helping others to enter fully into their unique, empowered, God-given life.

Lie Busters
verses
Your Truth

Seven Daily Messages About God's Truth for You

It's often hard to block out the negative messages we receive that lead us to believe we are not worthy, that we are hopeless, that we must drown in guilt and shame, that we are limited, unattractive, unable and ________ (you fill in the blank!). But these messages are not from God about the authentic, beautiful person he made you to be. The voice you hear whisper (or shout) these negative messages may come from a parent or others who influenced your childhood and, over time, they were easy to believe.

Over childhood and life experiences those lies become more real than the truth. It's hard to block out the automatic messages that come to the forefront of our thoughts and reflections. But God has given us the means to overcome the lies, big and small, that weave through our conscious thought. He did this by example – by sending Jesus to deliver His Word and live the life of extreme sacrifice, and to inspire those who followed in His footsteps to document and pass along the wisdom born of his human experience. The Bible is our guide to the Truth that God offers to us all – saint and sinner alike.

In His words and the deeds of Jesus and His generations of followers is the Truth we all need to live the life we were born to experience. God did not (could not) intend for us to be driven by lies we've encountered in our earthly journey. So, when you, or someone you care for, becomes overwhelmed by the false messages of our past, let me help you become open to God's Truth that is, by definition, good. He made you with a perfect plan that's exclusively for you. Elevate His voice above the negative chatter. Let His authentic plan guide your future.

Here are some of the lies we believe. Lies that keep us from our own, unique personal truth. Read your new message, memorize it and say it to yourself the moment your Lie creeps into your mind:

Lie 1: "I was an accident!"

Truth: God made everything with a place and a purpose..." *Proverbs 16:4*

The most profound example of this truth is in the life of Jesus. He was born with a powerful purpose, one that was destined to include the experience of the worst of humanity – pain, betrayal, injustice and agony. As God's son, Jesus knew where his path would lead and still he followed it to fulfill his God-given purpose. And the same is true for you and for me. Accept this beautiful truth in place of the lie. God makes no accidents!

New message to self:

I was intended, with a purpose and gifts given just to me.

Lie 2: "I can't do anything right."

Truth: "In his grace, God has given us different gifts for doing certain things well." *Romans 12:6*

We were each created with a unique and individual design. With special abilities, talents, gifts and personalities – like fingerprints on our souls. As humans we all make mistakes. Not one of us is perfect. God gave you the ability to do many things right and good. Actively embrace the gifts you received and nurture them. Excuse yourself for small imperfections. Romans 12:7-8 clearly explains how:

""If your gift is serving others, serve them well. If you are a teacher, teach well. If your gift is to encourage others, be encouraging. If it is giving, give generously. If God has given you leadership ability, take the responsibility seriously. And if you have a gift for showing kindness to others, do it gladly."

New message to self: I have unique gifts and abilities that will fulfill my purpose in life.

Lie 3: "I am too broken to be fixed."

Truth: "So if any man is in Christ, he is in a new world: the old things have come to an end; they have truly become new. "
2 Corinthians 5:17

Once we open our hearts and minds to God's truth, a new life becomes possible. No matter what we've done or how heinous our actions, how selfish or immoral we believe ourselves to be, God makes it clear you have His forgiveness. You are invited to a new start, an opportunity to live the life God intended for you. The most profound example of forgiveness came at the moment Jesus spoke from the cross and asked His Father to forgive His tormentors.

New message to self: I accept the opportunity offered through God's forgiveness to begin a new life according to His plan for me.

Lie #4: "No one will ever love me."

Truth: "Love bears all things, believes all things, hopes all things, endures all things. Love never ends...." 1 *Corinthians 13:4-8*

Bearing shame and guilt as a burden for things we have (or have not) done in the past makes us feel unworthy. Unworthy of opportunity. Unworthy of happiness. Unworthy of love. And this is the most damaging of all the lies we tell ourselves because love underlies everything in our lives – happiness, success, compassion for others and how we navigate the events in our lives. You were born with unqualified love imprinted on your soul. You didn't come with a set of "only if" stipulations like "Only if you don't use drugs, have an adulterous affair or __________ (insert your disqualifier)." No matter what you've done in your life that overwhelms you with doubt and pain, that imprint is there to stay. God loves you and you are therefore worthy of love – from yourself and from others.

New message to self: I will love myself as I love God's creation. I am worthy of love.

Lie #5: "If I can't have the real thing, a knock-off will do."

Truth: "If I speak in the tongues of men and of angels, but have not love, I am a noisy gong or a clanging cymbal." *Corinthians 13:1-3*

Our daily lives deliver a clear (though mistaken) message – if you can't afford (or be) the real thing, a knock-off will do. My own experience is a perfect example of this false assumption. I wanted to be a ballet dancer with the Bolshoi Ballet and I settled for being a stripper. I wanted a Burberry purse and bought fake with "pleather" straps instead of leather (bound to break in time). When we are not in touch with our authentic, God-given selves, we believe that we can manufacture our own 'real thing'. But a lie will never endure, never be satisfying. With time it will degrade and break and leave us with the pieces. The You that God brought into being is the genuine article – enduring, valuable and utterly unique.

New message to self: I am an authentic creation of God the Father, with a purpose that only I can fill through living a genuine life.

Lie #6: "I have no value, nothing to offer."

Truth: "Do not conform to the pattern of this world, but be transformed by the renewing of your mind. Then you will be able to test and approve what God's will is—His good, pleasing and perfect will." *Romans 12:2*

Carrying the regrets and secrets of the past on our backs weighs us down. We are unable to stand erect and face a better future. We are stuck in a pattern that's our living lie. But God endowed us with powerful and pliable minds so that we can adapt to new opportunities in life and renew our minds. We have the ability to move beyond the repetitive "I can't, I shouldn't" thoughts of the past and do God's will for us, embrace the gifts He's given us and leave the burdens of the past behind.

New message to self: I am one of God's valuable creations given the opportunity to change, grow and flourish.

Lie #7: 'I am too far gone to be saved.'

Truth: "... for all have sinned and fall short of the glory of God, and are justified freely by His grace through the redemption that is in Christ Jesus...." *Romans 3:23*

God doesn't weigh our sin on a scale. It's folly to compare the transgressions of our past with those of someone else's life in an effort to determine who is 'better or worse'. In the eyes of God drug addiction or prostitution is no greater a sin than another woman's gossip and judging. Forgiveness and redemption are offered equally to all who commit to walking in God's light. My past and yours are the same in His eyes.

New message to self: Like all of God's children I am never beyond His love and forgiveness.

A Final (Musical) Note

I've told you throughout my book of my love for music. I want to leave you with the lyrics of a beautiful song that expresses so many of the concepts I hope you'll embrace as you as unburden yourself and accept God's love. As you embrace the goodness and gifts that are yours by miraculous birth. As you reach out to others and invite them to walk in God's light alongside you. Just Come as You Are.

God Blessed you!

Amy Miranda

"Come As You Are"

By Ben Glover, David Crowder, Matt Maher

Come out of sadness
From wherever you've been.
Come broken hearted
Let rescue begin.
Come find your mercy
Oh sinner come kneel.
Earth has no sorrow
That heaven can't heal.
Earth has no sorrow
That heaven can't heal.

So lay down your burdens,
Lay down your shame.
All who are broken
Lift up your face.
Oh wanderer come home,
You're not too far.
So lay down your hurt,
Lay down your heart.
Come as you are.

There's hope for the hopeless
And all those who've strayed.
Come sit at the table,
Come taste the grace.
There's rest for the weary
Rest that endures.

So lay down your burdens,
Lay down your shame.
All who are broken
Lift up your face.
Oh wanderer come home,
You're not too far.
So lay down your hurt,
Lay down your heart.
Come as you are.

Fall in His arms
Come as you are.
There's joy for the morning,
Oh sinner be still.
Earth has no sorrow
That heaven can't heal.

So lay down your burdens,
Lay down your shame.
All who are broken
Lift up your face.
Oh wanderer come home,
You're not too far.
So lay down your hurt,
Lay down your heart.
Come as you are.

www.ingramcontent.com/pod-product-compliance
Lightning Source LLC
LaVergne TN
LVHW050940080826
845145LV00004B/1341
9780692999790